Sounds and Silences

Brenda Eldridge

Sounds and Silences

Acknowledgements

'Tapestry of Sound' was previously published in *Silver Cord*
'Assumptions' was previously published in *Not What They Night Seem*

Sounds and Silences
ISBN 978 1 76109 624 2
Copyright © text Brenda Eldridge 2023
Cover image: Atul Pandey from Unsplash

First published 2023 by
GINNINDERRA PRESS
PO Box 3461 Port Adelaide 5015
www.ginninderrapress.com.au

Contents

Ekphrastic Poetry	7
Tapestry of Sound	9
Lofty Thoughts	10
Spiegel im Spiegel	11
Pure Gold	12
Going Home	13
Frigid Silence	14
Ascending	15
Sparks Rising	16
Voices of Today	17
Moonrise	18
Snow	19
Generation Gap	20
Moonlight	22
Hatching	23
Voices on the Wind	24
Traditions	25
Spanish Nights	26
Harmony	27
Deep Silence	28
India	30
Not Quite Right	31
All There is to Know	32
Silence of Frustration	33
'Les Trois Cloches'	34
Sprechen ist Silbern Schweigen ist Golden	36
Whale Song	37
The Words We All Long to Hear	38
Windsong	39
Cascading	40

Sand Song	41
Swansong	42
Heartbeat	43
Power Released	44
Assumptions	45
Choosing Carefully	46
Comfortable Silence	48
Vibrato	49
Music to Our Ears	50
Song of the Bush	51
Don't Forget to Remember	52
Mysteries	54
Power of Prayer	55

Ekphrastic Poetry

For too many years
I believed mankind was incapable
of creating anything positive

Throughout history
all around me
was the evidence
that destruction was the thing
we were able to do best

I watched how nature revives
no matter what atrocities
we perform in the name of progress

Gradually I became aware
how important music was to me
all kinds of music
the melodic outpourings of birds
the simplest lullaby calming a fractious child
I noticed how notes deeply reverberating
dancing along the staves
or soaring skyward
expressed the feelings
I could put no name to

What I felt in my heart
and saw in my minds eye
had little to do with what
the composer might have envisioned

Music is ekphrastic poetry
we draw on our own experiences
to understand who we are
who we want to be

Tapestry of Sound

after Mahler, Symphony No. 5 in C Sharp Minor – 4. Adagietto

Strings blend harmonies
That take the spirit
In a flight
Soaring sweeping
Carelessly cascading

Drifting feather-like
Caught momentarily suspended
To roll like thunder
Ricocheting around the mountain tops
Reverberating in deep caverns

Plucking melodies
From the wind
Whispering, haunting
Weaving a tapestry of sound
With rainbow threads

Then airy as mist
Disappearing into nothing
Leaving only an echo
Gathering in the ether
To pour again

Lofty Thoughts

A rough path becomes the focus
taking care where I place each foot
for a single stone can send me tumbling
and as the years take their toll
even a light bump or graze
seems to hurt far more than when I was young

If I pause to catch my breath
I notice that sounds of other people
have become distant
and if I look down to the plain below
I feel the separateness

I hear more clearly a songbird trilling
the buzz of a passing fly or bee
the rattle of a rock that I had not touched
bringing a moment of angst of the unknown

I look up and the summit seems unreachable
but all I need to do is take one step at a time
feel the wind caress my hot face
know that I will soon be among the clouds

Spiegel im Spiegel

Arvo Pärt, *Mirror in the Mirror*

I don't know where images come from
and I have to smile to myself at life's incongruities

On hearing this piece a lifetime ago
having no idea what the title meant
I could imagine a spider doing press-ups on a mirror

Even now I am at a loss to know why
that image is the first I see
when I can also imagine a candle flame
reflected in a mirror
becoming flames glimmering beyond counting
warding off the darkness
sending it scurrying to far distant corners
perhaps not destroying it
but banishing it far enough away
for me to feel the peace within
that this simple playing of melodies
coming and going
like unsure lovers
gifts me

Pure Gold

I write that music is ekphrastic poetry

I cannot make beautiful music but
this morning I can hear a blackbird singing
and I reach out for a pen to start writing

He is on the other side of the tidal reach
I cannot see which branch he sits on
to present this world or a prospective mate
with such an outpouring –
liquid gold notes and trills
that lift my heart and senses

All else fades away

The niggling worries stop being overwhelming
I am free to sit by an open window
and drift on the ether
as airborne as his song
crossing not just the water
but years and miles
more than I want or need to count

Going Home

Antonín Dvořák, Symphony No. 9 (New World Symphony)

Somewhere over the years I heard
words put to this music,
all I remember is 'going home, I am going home'

Now as I listen to the haunting strains
I envision a skein of geese
in a pale dawn sky
huge birds with wide strong wings
beating the air rhythmically
they are going home with unerring accuracy

I am not one of their number
I have no migratory imprint
that tells me when I must take to the skies
watch lakes and mountains below
landmarks that will steer my course

Life called me away from my homeland
and I made a new life far away
not for me returning each year
I left without looking over my shoulder

I listen to the haunting oboe
and I want to cry
'take me home'
but I know home is not a place to go to
it is here within me
and I'm not sure what it is I hunger for
or am I feeling Dvořák's hunger rather than my own

Frigid Silence

I felt your dislike and mistrust
though not a word was said
shards of ice ricocheted across the room
gathering strength
I was surprised
I would have thought a direct look
would have been more lethal

My skin crawled
my heart struggled to maintain a beat
my mind was frozen
incapable of thought

And yes I was afraid for a while
until compassion saved me
and I wanted only to shield you
from the terrors of life
show you there was another way to love

Ascending

after Ralph Vaughan William, *Lark Ascending*

The Royal Albert Hall
Last Night at the Proms
Tasmin Little and her violin
set Vaughan Williams' lark free
from the page where George Meredith
had placed it with his words

No bird such as this could remain tethered
her liquid notes falling through the air
again and again
taking a listener back to sunny meadows
where once she lay on soft grass watching
a tiny black dot against a deep blue sky

Small wonder eyes filled with agony
lifted up to search the heavens
finding another lark
praying this song
hidden in the ether
would take a beloved soul safely home

Sparks Rising

There is a quiet only felt within the walls
of an old old house
where whispering echoes
of past tenants deepens the silence

A family sitting together
each lost in their own world
of dreams and imagination

Firelight sends shadows
dancing everywhere
and into this peace
logs settle with a soft sigh
sending sparks flying up the chimney
out into the darkness
to be as one
albeit briefly
with the stars

Voices of Today

after the Djari Project

Voice in suspended time
a slight huskiness
a quiver of age
the tremor of a tortured life
carefully accompanied by
an orchestra
young voices of a choir

Music has bridged
different cultures and histories
ancient tribes from distant lands
coming together
blended harmoniously
in the voices of today

Moonrise

For some there was interest
because it was a Super Blue Moon
a rare enough event
to warrant attention

Stephen knows my love of the moon
and every day searches the heavens
in case I have not seen her
I love to hear his voice from the top of the stairs
as he calls me to come and see…

Last night it was my turn to call him
and together we watched in stunned silence
as a full moon slipped above the darkened hills
as golden-orange as we have ever seen her

What need was there for music or words

Snow

Unlike rain with its gentle pattering
or urgent hammering
which brings us life itself
snow falls from heavy cloud
with no sound at all
and hides harsh reality

It covers everything with a purity
that turns ugliness to beautiful
and for a moment we can forget
misery and cold

Transport is brought to a standstill
telegraph wires break under its weight
and communications are disrupted
the world becomes magical
filled with mystery again

But most of all it brings a silence
borne of awe and wonder
and only the hardest of hearts
can ignore this gift of nature

Generation Gap

A cheerful tradie working on our balcony
had a Jimmy Barnes CD playing
the best way to hear it – loud

I found myself smiling
as years tumbled away
to when my teenage sons
as an act of rebellion against
John Denver and Steeleye Span
introduced me to Twisted Sister
Guns and Roses   KISS
Billy Joel and ABBA
and how could I ever forget
'Stairway to Heaven'

Their father was right
I was as lunatic as the boys
I loved 'You may be right, I may be crazy'
but I preferred the version by Alvin and the Chipmunks
as we all searched to find ourselves in music

I'm not sure they knew I played
Jimmy's 'Driving Wheels' VERY loud
when no one was around to witness

I am still caught by surprise and delight
by how well my sons know me
'I thought you'd like this, Mum…'
Disturbed performing 'Sounds of Silence'
at a live concert
much better than the gentle
Simon and Garfunkel recording
from long ago though the words
are as significant today as back when
I was a teenager

Moonlight

after Claude Debussy, *Clair de Lune*

Debussy first enchanted me
when in my teens
I would hear Clair de Lune
on the radio
little knowing he had been inspired
by a poem by Paul Verlaine

Before I knew its meaning
I painted a picture of what the music
conjured up within me –
high on a cliff overlooking the surging ocean
moonlight colouring everything
grey and silver among deep shadows

There was a sense of completion
when knowledge caught up with me

Hatching

As a child I watched in wordless wonder
when a hen strutted away from her nest
in search of lunch
leaving her clutch of eggs
golden brown and irresistible to touch

They were still warm from her body
and to my astonishment they moved –
only a little but unmistakable

I realised there was the faintest of tapping sounds
the chicks were beginning to peck their way
out of their homes
ready to come out into the big world

The shells cracked and a tiny form
fell out of each one
a black shining eye full of knowing
and big feet

Before my eyes they dried out
and became the fluffy chicks
I was familiar with
happy to sit in the palm of my hand

Miracles such as this were
a common part of life growing up on a farm
and I knew enough to be awestruck

Voices on the Wind

after 'The Skye Boat Song', adapted from a Gaelic folksong

History echoes in plaintive seagull cries
filled with haunting and heartbreak
a nations menfolk of all ages
fighting for survival
while their womenfolk
young and old
wail and keen for them
the loss of their homes and their homeland

Sounds of the oceans restless waves
drawn from the depths and the heights
of a piano keyboard and drums
a woman's voice soars above
calling calling
like the symbol of freedom
soon to be banished –
bagpipes with a voice like no other

Traditions

Listen to their music made from
what nature has gifted –
a straight branch carefully hollowed
and sticks tapped together

Listen how they echo this vast land
even vaster skies
the heat and precious water
wind   thunder   lightning
birds in flight
slithering snakes
leaping kangaroos
the comic and the dangerous

They lift their voices in harmony
uniting soul and creation

Spanish Nights

after Manitas de Plata

Flaming skies turn purple
vibrancy easing to darkness
different flames leap into the air
sending dark shadows running to hide
amid eager people gathered there

Flamenco guitarist begins to serenade
taking the throb of life from the dying day
blending it with the notes
an earthy sound that awakens desire

Gypsy dancers step out
lean sombrely clad men
holding themselves rigid controlled
their women all seductive movement
flashing their garish clothes
inner fire entices from careful disdain

A crescendo is reached
tension broken
passion replete
in the steps of the dance

The guitarist litters the night
with a soft gentle melody
that drifts to nothing

Harmony

For years I hungered
for one I could share my life with
a like-minded soul…
and a set of wind chimes

Both yearnings have been satisfied

Stephen is my heart's delight –
we sit under the veranda
for morning coffee
chatting and laughing softly
about this and that
as we watch the birds flitting
about the garden

Beside us are the wind-chimes
their stand is almost as tall as I am –
(some harsh person could say
that isn't very high)
long metal pipes hang sedately
which can clank discordantly
or like today
with a slight breeze
gently hum long long notes
almost impossible to know
when they have run their course
and only our voices are left
and the birds

Deep Silence

In a forest of enormous trees
we carefully entered a partially hidden cave
climbed down steep steps and along a narrow path
noting first the drop in temperature
how quickly it felt damp cold
even though there were no drafts

It was this stillness that held us

Clever lighting enhanced the miracles
of stalagmites and stalactites

Huge waves of rock they call shawls
spikes and spires that make you think
of the cathedrals they are named after

A glisten of moisture lingers
at the top of a stalagmite
fed by the long finger of rock
descending from above
and will become part of the massive growth
and in time
a column of unknown strength

As we stood entranced
the silence felt like a weight
bared tree roots reminding us
of the world in the daylight outside

A tinkle of a drop of water landing
in a puddle
broke the silence
as if breaking a spell

India

I have started a new tapestry
which has taken me to India
with its exotic sounds and colours

The peacock I will embroider
stares at me from the picture
with an intense gaze
and my eyes look at the rich
blues and greens of its plumage
and wonder where we will go together
over the next months

Already I can hear a piercing wailing song
full of half-notes and unexpected vibrato
rising high over the noise of people on the move
with the intricate fluid notes of a sitar
holding it aloft as well as keeping it grounded

I see a white egret at twilight
silently climbing the air with slow beating wings
heading for a tranquil lake shrouded in mist
a place of complete contrast
for a departing soul to find rest

I see sacred mountains
clothed in snow
coloured pink and gold by a rising sun
I seek forgiveness for the desecration
by shallow tourists clambering uncaring
amongst the grandeur
leaving behind filth and detritus

Not Quite Right

after *633 Squadron* theme by Ron Goodwin

In my teens a piece of music
was often played on the radio

It caught my attention –
I could see Spanish galleons
on tumultuous seas
almost feel the wind and salt spray
I could sense the drama
the anticipation of the unknown…

It was quite a shock to learn
it was the theme music
for a movie called *633 Squadron*
and was nothing to do with sailing ships
rather planes and resistance fighters
in Norway during World War II

I was curious to hear it again
after so many years
I found something on YouTube
watched the opening scenes
felt the jolt as the music played
and my eyes saw planes
but my mind still saw galleons…

All There is to Know

I love how flutes take me by the hand
and lead me astray
away from common sense and sensible
gently dropping me into a world filled
with fantasy and things that might be
or might not…
where I can decide

The golden notes played by James Galway
took me into Tolkien's world
of Hobbits who saved Middle Earth

The impossible made possible
by faith and strength
by brave hearts prepared
to do all that they must
to save all that is good

I recall the words of Gandalf
'You can learn all there is to know
about their ways in a month
and yet after a hundred years
they can still surprise you at a pinch'

And it was written that Hobbits
are a lot like people…

Silence of Frustration

I long to be able to silence
the words in my head

Words I rage at those who seem obtuse
while they are hurting people I love

Conversations had with no resolution
of ideas or conflict

I live my life in the knowledge
I do the best I can with every day
I must allow others this same latitude
and remember I have little idea
why they do or say the things they do

Sometimes the silence of frustration
is the beginning of new wisdom

'Les Trois Cloches'

A success for Les Compagnons with Edith Piaf, 1946

A French song about bells tolling
to announce the birth – marriage – death
of one of a small community living hidden
in a tree-filled valley…

The words of the song are universal
lives acknowledged by the chiming of bells

A single bell calling the faithful to prayer

A glorious cascading peal ringing out
to celebrate the end of war
and a blessing of marriage vows

A solitary bell ringing mournfully
when someone dies –
a chime for each year lived

On board a ship the bell is rung
eight times before midnight
and eight times after
to farewell the old year and
welcome the new

To bell ringers they are old friends
loved with ardent dedication
as ropes are pulled in strict formation
aggravations of ordinary life forgotten
bringing a sense of deep unity

A lone bell ringing touches a heart
and a spirit quietens in contemplation

Sprechen ist Silbern Schweigen ist Golden

Translated by Thomas Carlyle to 'Speech is Silver, Silence is Golden'

I remember the song 'Silence is Golden'
from the UK 60s music era
when someone used to sing this to me

In my callow youth I did not understand
the fuller import of the message

Now I know the pain of standing by
watching what is happening to those I love
knowing that I – with my love of words
to express joys and sorrows
to open other hearts and minds
to things I have learned –
must stay silent

Words have more power than we can ever know
once they have passed over a tongue
they cannot be unsaid

When trust is betrayed by words
can it be like a broken bone
stronger in the place where it has healed itself
to be given again
or will it ever be surrounded and
protected by caution
stunted and shivering
like a battered and bewildered child

Whale Song

We were standing on a grassy bank
overlooking the ocean
a short distance away several whales
were leaping clear of the water
leaving a wake of rainbow-filled mist
breath-taking in majesty
the sheer joy of living

Closer by in a sheltered bay
mother and child languished
softly singing to each other
huge yet so gentle…

I had never heard anything like it
as they embraced me with their song
I longed to be with them
be a physical part of their unity

My vision was blurred by unshed tears
and with an aching heart
I was left wondering as I still do
if people have experienced this perfect connection
with their newborn children
why is it the world is
the way it is

The Words We All Long to Hear

after Cole Porter, 'In the Still of the Night', 1937

All lovers have a signature tune
a lyricist writing the words
we long to say and long to hear
but don't have the artistry
aren't able to magic a melody from the ether
that plucks our heartstrings
creating a harmony echoing our feelings
encapsulating our hopes and dreams
of now and the future

We have such a song –
we played it at our wedding
a joyous occasion shared with
family and friends eleven years ago
or was it yesterday
and it can still bring tears to our eyes
as we whisper the questions and answers
renewing our promises
each time we hear it

Windsong

I watched my sons go up in a glider
as part of their air force cadet training
and knew an unexpected longing

Their father could be a thoughtful man
and he arranged for me to go up

Much to everyones surprise I think
I loved being separate from the earth below
I witnessed the sunset
as a mass of custard-yellow swirling clouds
over the sea

The silence I had anticipated
did not happen

It was the steady whistle of the wind
that gifted us musical accompaniment

Cascading

after Chris Botti

A trumpet playing 'The Last Post'
stills my heart as tears well
not always to fall
unlike the notes that cascade
as unique phrasing of familiar melodies
breathes new life into them
a style instantly recognised
once you have heard him

Notes pure and clean
held for long moments
then the silence – exactly right
before the next carefully released
flood of music brings the listener
safe back to shore

Sand Song

Not all sand is the white of our local beach
that hisses when a southerly wind blows
hurling hard granules at my face
stinging my cheeks
getting stuck between my teeth
making my eyes water in protest

We found different dunes far from a sea
coloured delicate shades of pink sandstone
powder soft to clamber up
each footstep slipping and sliding
reaching a summit only to find
another dune rolling away
with an equally pristine horizon
against a clear blue sky

Long trailing strands of paddy melon
lay decoratively as if carefully draped
a small stand of old gum trees
shrouded in cobwebs and curls of bark
hanging like forgotten washing

I didn't know silence could be a warmth
created by the air and a gentle heat
radiating from the sand itself
it felt like sacrilege to speak
to intrude our thoughts
no matter how profound

Swansong

after Richard Strauss

Who among us would not like
to end our lives on a high note

To spend a lifetime creating
music that touches the hearts of many
that goes down in recorded history
despite fire flood famine and wars

In those dying months
of a life of over eight decades
to be able to compose four last songs
a personal tribute to a life well lived
raptures of simplicity and sublime artistry
before going to the place
there is no returning from
leaving an incomparable legacy

Heartbeat

Cradled in a perfectly formed cocoon
an unborn child waits and grows

A mother might sing lullabies
or listen to relaxing music
believing the little one will be soothed
she might have food fancies
and say it is the baby needing
the taste of apricots and pickled onions

Not even the most loving mother-in-waiting
really knows what her child feels or needs
or what it is like within her womb

There is only one certainty –
it is her own steady heartbeat
sustaining and nourishing life

Power Released

Van Halen playing for the movie *Twister*

The growl of his guitar
conjures up the deep menace
of a tornado
with impossibly dark clouds
building and building in strength
sending down a finger of power
to devastate

With energy almost spent
he creates a golden arc of sound
soaring upward as if the tornado
wails at its own demise

And those still standing on the ground
physically and emotionally
buffeted and ravaged
are hoping the brooding silence
will deter the return of more destruction

Assumptions

He was busking by the shopping-centre door
Not someone to argue with lightly
Tall with hefty broad shoulders
Large pot belly covered
In an old grey T-shirt
Shaved head and tattoos
A long grey grizzled beard

Easy to link him with the Harley
Parked nearby
Not so easy to link him
With the delicate honeyed notes
Pouring from the flute he was playing

Choosing Carefully

We choose so carefully
the music played at the funeral
of one dear to us

Their going makes us think
of times laughter and tears shared
we recognise the depth of
how precious they are to us
and always will be

Some cultures do not speak of the dead
forbid the use of their name
I am not of that culture
I need to talk of my loved ones
share memories with others
who knew them
it is how I keep them in my life
as if for moment I could forget

Southern Sons sang 'Hold Me in Your Arms'
a love song for some
for this mother whose arms were torn and gone
they were a plea –
'You my beloved son don't forget me'

You were learning to appreciate the classics
and I was quietly pleased when you said
you liked Beethoven's *Für Elise*
I had this played for you too
not thinking I would hear it again and again
every time I used the photocopier at work

I was found weeping there many times
but comforted all the same

Comfortable Silence

A lifetime longing for comfortable silence
not the embrace of solitude
the silence shared with a like-minded soul

I knew we had this during the long hours in hospital
when surgery robbed Stephen of speech
but there was no angst between us

He rested
following his own thoughts to recovery
I sat and wrote poetry or read

Years later here we sit together in the cosy corner
the soft hum of the fridge in the background
sunshine pouring in through the window

He does a cryptic crossword or reads
sipping a glass of aged Riesling
relishing the peace and tranquillity

I stop my embroidery – the peacock will wait
while I capture these moments
this comfortable silence we are blessed with

Vibrato

after Dolly Parton, 'From Here to the Moon and Back'

A new person comes into our lives
and brings with them
things we would never have thought
we would learn to enjoy

Oh be still my heart for I
have loved the voice of Kris Kristofferson
for many years
and when he recorded a song with Dolly Parton
I was captivated…
and so was Stephen
whose taste runs more to the classics and jazz

Kris doesn't do it for Stephen
but he does like the vibrato
inherent in Dolly's voice
and who with an ounce of romance in their soul
would not be entranced
by being loved to the moon and back

Music to Our Ears

The bastard cancer haunts our beautiful lives

Thirteen years ago it tried to take Stephen away
with its sneak attack –
not an ulcer in his gum –
something life-stealing

Clever surgery cut it out
leaving a narrow margin of safety
so each year we present ourselves to the hospital
for the check-up
only releasing our held-in breath
when the specialist cheerfully says
'All clear' and we step out into the sunlight again

Not so simple this year –
'What is this?'

Weeks passed in excruciating misery and dread

The heart-stopping biopsy – and more waiting

The hard question
'What do we do if the bastard cancer is back?'

Then music to our ears
'All clear – see you in three months –
just to be sure…'

Song of the Bush

In the heart of Kakadu
miles from man-made civilisation
sitting in a silent boat
in the middle of a river

Cliffs towered to one side and ahead
rugged and lichen-covered against a blue sky
to the other side trees
trees and more trees

We were embraced by life
the gentle churr of hidden insects
a blip on the waters surface
a little fish not a big crocodile
a rustle among tall reeds
a lone bird calling
the steady beat of our hearts
linking us to all creation

Don't Forget to Remember

written by Barry and Maurice Gibb, 1969

I hear the Bee Gees singing
and I am thrust back to England in the 60s –

My dad loved the songs of this era
I think for a few hours on Sunday afternoons
he felt as young as his teenage children
as our home was filled
with the sounds of *Top of the Pops*

Suddenly he is right here with me
I can hear his voice
see how he stood – shoulders slightly hunched over
shirtsleeves rolled up to above his elbows
forearms burned and weathered
from working in the fields
sun-bleached hair and high forehead
the inevitable cigarette – which killed him in the end

How can my mind take in
that I haven't seen him
felt his arms around me
for over fifty years

He died forty years ago on 29 September
local tradition set this date
as the one when the harvest must be in
Mother always said he lingered to be part of the harvest –
he was only sixty

He is the blood in my veins
and in the music

Mysteries

Misty mornings of veiled sunlight
before warmth dries the air
and moisture from grasses and leaves

A loch perfectly still
reflects surrounding mountains
a moored yacht
everything poised waiting to begin a new day

Fog eerily sending grey fingers
among ancient beeches
making silver tree trunks more mysterious
a stillness that hides the unnameable
a snap of a twig
sending tendrils of disquiet
across the skin of a passer-by
who picks up the pace
and hurries home to light a comforting fire

Familiar tidal reach rendered strange
sea mist has come down
and hidden the opposite shore
apartment buildings have disappeared
posts where pelicans perch are gone
no sound of lapping waves against rocks
we could be cast adrift on a wide sea
and not know where we are
or where we might be going –
a lot like life really

Power of Prayer

Step through the portals of an old church
and it is to step into the power of prayer –
centuries of whispered voices
entreating a higher being for
comfort   strength   support

The silence is profound
it does not need the help
of exquisite choral harmonies
a choir boy's pure voice soaring
held aloft by deep male tones
the intricacies of an organ

You can sit here and be embraced
by the prayers of the faithful
and be elevated on their wings
when you have no words of your own

www.ingramcontent.com/pod-product-compliance
Lightning Source LLC
Chambersburg PA
CBHW071037080526
44587CB00015B/2659